TALES

OF A

GLASGOW

CARPET FITTER

i

Tom laird

ii

TALES

OF A

GLASGOW

CARPET FITTER

BY

Tom Laird

ISBN: 9798732041057

Cover Design

Tom Laird

ACKNOWLEDGEMENTS

I would first like to pay a mark of respect to my deceased brother-in-law **John Hood**, Author of **The History Of Clydebank** and among many other publications, who inspired me before he passed away, 6th Dec 2018. He gave me plenty of encouragement. He always said "You should write a book, I'm sure you've got lots of stories to tell. Well, I have taken your advice John and dived right in with this my first book.

Finally, I would like to thank my wife Marion who worked with me 24/7 from the nineties until we retired. She knows the background to a lot of these stories, having experienced them with me. During lockdown I made a video for my family and then proceeded with this book. I'd like to thank the person that did the illustrations, but nobody is owning up, I'm afraid it was me. I'm a carpet fitter not an artist, I'm sure you'll agree.

CONTENT

INTRODUCTION

It all started for me when I joined Templeton Carpet Factory in Bridgeton in the east end of Glasgow when I was 17. They started me in the dyehouse, which involved wool hanks that were put through the dyeing process and taking them to be tested. I was there for about two months, before they moved me on to being a chute boy which entailed collecting broadloom carpets that had come off the looms on the 1st floor and were sent down a chute, hence the name.

We would then take the carpet along to the broadloom hall where it would be rolled and elevated up on a large forklift boom type crane and installed into a space in the storage racks, which if I remember right were about six or seven tiers high. After doing this job for about six or seven weeks I was moved on to the jute dept. This where the jute used to come in from Dundee, from here it proceeded to the beaming where they it would prepare it for weaving.

I was beginning to think that I wasn't suitable for any of the jobs and when I was called to the personnel office, I didn't know what to expect. Turned out they offered me a job which had just been created for me in the seaming dept. This was where I started to learn all the various stages of seaming and joining carpets together and what you could do to them to make them match i.e.,(stretching/shrinking).

I started to learn how to fit carpets properly. The seaming dept. was moved from the top floor to the ground floor made which made more sense logistically, making things easier and more accessible. My pal Robert who worked on the cropping machines which can be described as (like a lawnmower that is fitted into a machine). We decided to go to Jersey to work. After a couple of weeks, we managed to get a job painting only to be fired at the end of the week. I ran out of money and came back the following day, Robert stayed on he had more money than me. Templeton heard I was back and offered me my job back,

I should have, but I didn't answer. It was about a year and a half later after working in England and getting married, my wife and I moved back to Scotland, desperate for a job. I tried Templeton again, I got my old job back working with my new boss Jimmy.

After I started back Jimmy asked if I wanted to work after hours fitting carpets with him, which I agreed to do. He used to get a lot of work from people in the factory and the office depts. We used to work two or three nights a week. Eventually we started to get work from a shop in Castlemilk, Coulters the drapers who had started selling carpets. This kept us busy and after a period of time we decided to Leave Templeton and work for ourselves in a partnership. We decided to call the business Glendale Carpets. Before We started Jimmy invited his cousin John to join us. For me this lasted a year.

I wasn't getting regular income on time and started to fall behind with bills, so I left. Over the years I have had other jobs, but the carpet fitting was always a part of my life. Later in 1987 I formed my own business, Laidwel Carpet Services which I ran for about 16 successful years..

CASTLEMILK DOLLY

In the early days of my fitting career, we went to fit a bedroom carpet in a house in Castlemilk. In those days it was mostly Axminister carpets that were mainly the only choice for the working families who could afford them, that, or linoleum, that was mostly made in Kirkcaldy, and was the poor man's choice with a rug on top to make it feel a bit warmer.

Anyway, this woman was getting an Axminister carpet fitted, accompanied with a heavy hair underlay. In those days, the carpets were fitted using carpet tacks and the felt underlay with a hammer staple gun. This was before cheaper carpets came along. So, it took a while to do the whole procedure, longer than it takes nowadays with gripper and all the built-in underlays and foam backs, with the latter being less common now. We were just finishing off the fitting, when the woman chapped on the bedroom door, Jimmy opened it to hear her wee lassie greeting and asking had we seen the weans doll. Jimmy said "no, we hadn't", and queried "what size it was?

The woman answered, "och it was only a wee one, it was her favourite". Jimmy said, "sorry we've not seen it" and closed the door to the screams of the wean. We started slowly scouring the room and then refusing to acknowledge a little bump that was below the carpet that must have been under the felt. Jimmy lifted the hammer, and aggressively repeatedly battered the bump whispering

AGAIN! I'M NO FUCKIN LIFTING ALL THIS

TAKE THE BISCUIT

One of the earliest memorable jobs, which was privately booked and not from the various contacts that we had built up. It was a beautiful old Victorian mansion in Strathaven sitting on the perimeter of the town. We arrived quite early in the morning about 8.30 a.m. as it was a large hall, stairs and landing as well as a more than adequate sitting room. The first thing that struck me when the woman opened the door was her resemblance to Rita Tushingham the actress.

When I told my wife later that night, she replied "not again, you're always saying people look like some celebrity when they're not". I suppose I have got a habit of doing that, anyway that is not what this story is about, so back to the job. We had been working all morning and this was now about 2 p.m. I was getting that fain feeling and dry throat sort of way, when you have had nothing in your stomach, the woman (Rita, we'll call her), asked if we would like a cup of tea and something to eat? right away we shouted "yes please" above the noise of the hammering.

After fifteen long minutes, that's what it felt like she called us into the kitchen. As we entered the room and sat at the table, I had this vision of food like a mirage in my mind and what it was going to be like. Rita came over to the table with fancy china and presented us with 2 cups of tea and 4 cream crackers. I thought, small mercies but I was so desperate to get anything into my mouth that there was no disappointment in what I saw. Jimmy was already into his second cracker, as I devoured my first, when a small hand appeared above the table heading in the direction of the last cracker.

With an immediate reaction I slapped the plate removing the cracker and straight into my mouth. All hell broke loose, screaming and jumping up and down on the floor was the owner of the hand, Rita's wee boy. She ran into the kitchen shouting, "what's wrong with him", Jimmy and I both at the same time mumbling **"don't know"**, withs bits of crackers being expelled from our mouths.

6

WRANG WINDAES

Over the fifty years that I have been fitting carpets, I developed and diversified the number of services that I was offering. This meant I was either the main contractor or subcontractor depending on what company or local council I was working for. This particular job I was subcontracting to a Joinery firm, who my company did initial cleans for.

They were doing a refurbishment in a local whisky distillery building that used to be

7

used as the old canteen. The joinery firm asked us if we could clean the windows as well and said we would need ladders. Well at the time we only carried step ladders with us, so I asked the guy who used to clean windows in houses across from my house. I told him it was worth £50.00 to him if he was interested, which he agreed to do.

I gave him the details and told him to meet two of my workers there at a certain time. I had three jobs on the go at the same time, so I could not personally be there, and would turn up later. Later on, I got a phone call from one of my workers saying they couldn't find the building in question, they had asked security and they hadn't a clue.

I asked her if the window cleaner had turned up and she said yes, he is standing here, so I said, "tell him to wait till we get there". When we arrived there, I asked where the window cleaner was, to be told he would not wait, so we carried on and

finished the job when I found out where the actual building was in the grounds. As it turned out we managed to clean the windows using our stepladders. Later that night there was a chap at the door and opened it to find the window cleaner standing arms open wide saying "Well did I do a good job?". My workers asked you to stay and you went away, and we did them"",
I said, "No", he says I cleaned the canteen, I asked somebody where it was, there were other people cleaning the windows, so I joined them. So, have you got my £50,00, I replied,

"WRANG CANTEEN, WRANG WINDAES,"
and shut the door
WELL DID I DO A GOOD JOB

9

AIRMAIL

This memory is still very vivid in my mind. One of the various heating contractors that we used to do lots of work for, by either going the previous day or first thing in the morning (8.00 a.m.) to gain access to the property in question and loosen the carpets at different areas in the rooms or hall of the house that the heating engineers needed access to. This one was 8.00 a.m.

We would usually turn up at the address about 15 minutes before we could go in, the gas fitters would either be there before us or just after us. Turns 8 o'clock, and the gas fitters have not arrived yet, so we go up and chap the door, wait a couple of minutes, no answer. We try again, this time a woman's voice answers, "Whit is it" we reply, "carpet fitters to loosen your carpets for the central heating installation". She replies, "am no wantin it", we say "it has been arranged", she shouts back "yer no getting in".

We headed back down the stairs to the van just as the gas fitters turned up. "Is that it ready then?" they said. "No, she won't let us in, she doesn't want it". "Aye that'll be right, no way" as we headed up the stairs again to the door. With a really heavy chap to the door and rattling the letterbox at the same time, shouting "gas fitters for the central heating", next minute the door opens slightly but not letting anybody in the same woman says, " I don't want it", gas fitter replies, "but you've got to----", the door **SLAMS!** shut with the woman shouting, "I don't fuckin want it" and the letterbox came flying off the door at what looked like a hundred miles an hour.

We retired to our vans, gas fitters phoned their office, who in turn phoned the council, and they duly phoned the woman who came out to tell us we could go in. Surprisingly, everything went ok, even when we went back the next day to relay them.

Amazingly the letterbox had been reinstalled.

CONSERVATORY SECRET

Back in the late 80's or was it the early 90's we got a call to give a quote for fitting a carpet in a conservatory in a big house in the Riddrie area. After agreeing a price, we arranged to fit the carpet the following week when it was due to be delivered. Next week we arrived at the house to be taken into the conservatory.

What the woman didn't say, when she phoned for the price, was that we had to lift the old carpet and underlay, so after readjusting the price for the job we proceeded to lift the carpet. When we started to lift the underlay at one corner which the carpet had also been loose at, was a girlie magazine, a lesbian type of magazine. So, the dilemma was who do we tell? the woman or the man or both.

We knew it couldn't have been a previous owner, as the magazine was modern looking. This indeed got us thinking not to say anything and take it away with us,(don't bother I can imagine what you're thinking). In the end we fitted the new underlay and carpet and decided to save a marriage and placed the magazine back under the underlay at the same corner, only this time they will have to loosen the carpet at the corner.

Fortunately, it was fitted with a smooth edge installation, and the conservatory secret was preserved,

IS YOUR MITHER NO COMING

This was a private job that I had booked over the phone, I remember it well, it was at the time when my sister and her husband came back from South Africa to stay with us for a few days before they moved to Ireland to retire there. Well, that is not the main reason, as I tell the story all will be revealed. Let us say her name was Alice for privacy reasons and she stayed in Milngavie. It was a Saturday morning and I said goodbye to my sister and her man saying we would see them later.

Any way we found the house (we meaning), my wife and I who started working with me in the early 90's), and rang the doorbell, It was answered by Alice who beckoned us into the house. Previously on the phone she told us she had just moved into the house, and it was the living room, bedroom, hall that she wanted carpets fitted, and vinyl in the kitchen and bathroom, so it was a lucrative job for us and at the time and we weren't all that busy. As a matter of fact, things were very quiet and normally

I would not have taken the job as my sister was staying with us just for a few days, but needs must, so we had to bite the bullet. Anyway, back to the task in hand. We proceeded to start preparing the floor and start fitting the carpets. The only piece of furniture in the house was a single bed in Alice's room which she was lying on.

After a while she got up and went outside and returned about 10 minutes later carrying a carrier bag and disappeared into the bedroom closing the door behind her. I finished fitting the living room carpet and started working in the hall. It must have been the banging on the floor that caused the bedroom door to open slightly, there was a bottle of cider by the side of her bed'

I told Marion my wife what she was doing. It must have been about a half hour later that the bedroom door flies open, and a fleeting figure runs across the hall into the kitchen. All hell breaks loose, screaming, shouting, and crying, we run to the kitchen, Alice standing there, blood running from her wrist holding a Stanley knife in her other hand. Thank god Marion was with me and she knew what to do, she wrapped a cloth around her wrist to suppress the flow. I dialled 999 and told them what happened, they said an ambulance will be there ASAP.

19

About 5 minutes later it turned up along with the police given the nature of what had happened. They started questioning me about where she got the knife, implying it belonged to us. I in turn told them that she had got it in the kitchen and must have used it when wallpapering the rooms

. Satisfied with that assumption they left it at that. Alice's mother turned up before she was taken away by the ambulance. She was apologetic for Alice's behaviour, explaining that she had just come out of hospital where she was being treated for mental health issues, asking could we come back maybe on Monday if it was suitable. I replied, "I'd have to think about it, and could she pay us for the work we had done, and only if she was going to be there", only then would it be considered. "Yes, I'll definitely be there," she replied.

We got back to our house where we relayed the story to my sister and her man, who could not believe it. Next day, Sunday night the phone rings. Marion picked up the phone and said "it is Alice that's on the line, asking if we could come back and finish the work in her house" she was profusely apologizing for what happened. I was reluctant to give her an answer, hesitatingly saying I would only come if her mother was going to be there till, we finish the job.

She assured us she would be, so we told her we would be there 9.00 a.m. We arrived Monday morning. Alice opened the door and invited us in with me asking "is your mother here Alice?", with her replying "Yes she is coming". It was going to take us at least another two to three hours to finish. I kept asking her if the mother was definitely coming, "OH YES, she's coming" she said ". She came out of the kitchen holding two cakes, saying "I made these for the two of you, I was, looking at Marion dubiously, and thanking Alice at the same time.

21

I eventually gave up asking about her mother, but I couldn't help wondering where she was, after all she assured us, she was going to be there. As I was finishing off the hall carpet, my gaze kept being drawn towards the fridge/freezer in the kitchen, with visions of the mother's head on a shelf staring out at me, as the door creaked open. Stop it I thought to myself, but the vision would not go away.

Eventually I had to fit the vinyl in the kitchen, I had been leaving it to the last, dreading it, so we moved the fridge carefully and completed the job. Got paid and got out of there as quickly as we could, no pleasant goodbyes nothing. Arriving back at our house my sister enquired how we got on, "was she alright" she said,

I replied "yes, we were only glad
to get out of there"

GOD WORKS IN MYSTERIOUS WAYS

This story relates to the time I had a contract with the housing dept. In Castlemilk. Alongside the other contracts we had going at the time we were supplying and fitting carpets in flats in Castlemilk for the people that were decanted out of their houses while they were being refurbished. These flats were flats that were lying empty and were used for temporary accommodation. That day we had been particularly busy, so I decided to pick up the carpets and deliver them, that afternoon as they were being fitted the next morning.

Normally we fit them when we deliver them but as I said we were terribly busy. These empty flats usually have metal doors fixed to them to stop any vandalism and are removed the day of occupation. I would pick up the keys for these flats to measure them and then install the carpets. Anytime we delivered these carpets, especially if it's the day before the installation, we would try to get in and out as in short, a time as possible so as not to draw any attention to us or the fact that we're putting carpets into an empty flat and leaving them.

So, when we turned up at the address, the street wasn't that busy. The house was on the top floor, so we were not looking forward to carrying them up the stairs, not when it's five carpets and two-part rolls of vinyl. As we started to empty the van, with

Marion being left behind to watch the cargo we proceeded up the stairs.

While we were doing that, two men dressed in black approached Marion and started talking to her, she told them that we very busy and she didn't have time, and they asked if they could help. By this time, myself and Jim who was working with us got down the stairs. I was wondering what these guys were doing talking to my wife. When I asked, "what's up Marion?" she said, "they offered to help".

Not being sure what they were up to I thought better where I can see them rather than leave them with Marion, I said "sure" much appreciated" and they grabbed a carpet and headed up the stairs in front of us, as I said I wasn't sure what they were up to. Well after the delivery was completed, I said thanks very much to the two guys who were standing and wanting to talk, "sorry guys we don't really have the time, thanks again". I Got into the van and drove away to see them with the sun in my rear-view mirror as black silhouettes that made me realise,

THEY WERE MORMONS! SO, I

THOUGHT TO MY SELF,THANK YOU GOD.

DUKE ST. HOSPITAL

Back in 1972 my wife was expecting our second child and was admitted to the hospital when she started to experience labour pains and thought the baby was to emerge, not like before when she gave birth to our son who seemed to take forever, and she had to be induced. Unfortunately, our daughter had to be put in an incubator because she was jaundiced, subsequently she was kept in for a few days. One day I was going to go up to visit Marion and "Denise" is what we named her.

28

My Da wanted to come as well so after work I picked him up before we went back to my house, which was a room and kitchen we were staying in at the time. Anyway, I left my Da in the living room as I hurried through to the bedroom, which was a bit of a mess with Marion being in hospital I had let things fall behind, including a rolled-up carpet which because of lack of space I had to walk on to the chest of drawers to get a change of clothes.

When I went back through to the living room, my Da said "where's wee Jimmy?" (that was our budgie), "he's not in his cage". "Oh, I let him out sometimes when I'm out, to give him a bit of freedom". (Actually this is how I met wee Jimmy). I was out in my milk round in Queenslie, I heard a commotion coming from the trees in the janitor's garden of the local school. It was a wee blue budgie being harassed by sparrows. I managed to encourage him down onto the fence and got him to approach my outstretched finger mimicking a perch. He hopped on and I closed fingers around his claws.

I managed to put him into an empty milk crate until I got him home, stopping at a pet shop on the way to buy a cage. So that is story how I got him,) "I don't have time, I'll look for him later. I hope he's no went up the chimney", I said. So, we proceeded to the hospital and my Da saw Denise. Marion was full of question" how is the house, everything ok. have you put the new carpet down yet?". "No, I'll do it tomorrow," I said.

The carpet had been lying in that room before she went into hospital, so that was the next thing on the list of things to do. At this particular time in my life, with me working as a milkman, so it was an early rise, and I usually had a wee sleep when I came home. When I got back from work that day, I thought I better get that carpet fitted, Because it had been lying for so long and with me using it as a shortcut it went into an oval shape with walking on it tends to flatten and it harder to get the creases out,

I just made it harder for myself. As I unrolled it awkwardly because of the shape, there appeared Wee Jimmy completely flattened like a pressed flower. I forgot to look for him, he must have been having a wee stroll through the carpet when I walked along it. Poor wee soul how was I going to tell my Da who loved him. He used to like nibbling my Da's ear

At least he lived for about a year, longer than he would have if the sparrows had got him.

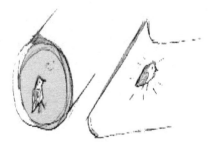

IT'S NO MINE

This is a job we were doing for one of the heating firms that had contracts all over Scotland, mostly the central belt and east of Scotland. This job was in Duntocher. That is where my wife was brought up, although she was born in Old Kilpatrick just down the road from there, where we were also working.

We chapped on the door of this house that was next door to the one she used to live in. This was the day before the heating engineers were coming. The woman opened the door, and we explained that we

33

were to loosen the carpets for the heating engineers the next morning, she invited us in, and we proceeded to work through all the rooms, that only left the hall and the top landing.

It was when we were lifting the top landing carpet that we came across a bank book, which had been sneakily squeezed under a corner of the carpet in an area that had been under a Piece of furniture. I showed it to my wife saying, "what we are going to do?", as by this time the woman's husband had come in and we didn't know who it belonged to. We just

went for gold and said that we had found it under the carpet. They both looked at one another, not shedding any light on whose it was.

There was an eerie silence between them and the odd glare. We finished the job in hand saying we would be back in two days

34

to relay them.   As we left the house, I was thinking we had just left what was going to become a **war zone**. When we returned to relay the carpets there was no comments from the woman, and no sign of her husband and no word of thanks for finding the bankbook or who owned it,

OR HAD SHE KICKED HER HUSBAND OOT

I'LL PRAY FOR YOU

We did work for a furniture shop near the Barras which was mostly domestic work, but they had successfully won a contract for supplying furniture, curtains, and carpets for homeless flats, amongst other contracts that they procured. One was linked to a building firm that had a contract with RBS to refurbish flats that had been repossessed across Scotland. This job had been passed to a building firm in Manchester.

It was a total of five houses that had to be fitted out with carpets and vinyl and because of the distance we were also asked to install window blinds, which were usually put up by the team that worked for the shop.

There was a total of eighteen carpets and ten cuts of vinyl and of course the blinds. There was no way my long wheelbase transit was going to be able to carry all that, so I discussed it with the furniture shop owner who agreed that he would have to hire a Luton type van. The job was starting on the Monday of the following week and scheduled to last five days. It was arranged that I meet the builder on Monday at 2.30 p.m. in Manchester.

I had also been told to pick up the hired van first thing that Monday at a place in Dennistoun. I could not think of any hire firms in that area, I only knew where the main hire firms were. Anyway, we made our way and found the garage and proceeded to the reception where I was met by the owner. I told him I was there to pick up the van that had been booked in my name. He asked when I would return it and I replied, "Friday or Saturday".

He sent us out to the yard to see the mechanic and get the keys. It turns out I knew the mechanic, his name was Sammy, who had previously done work for me on a van I used to own. "Hi how are you"? he asked, "fine, hope that's a good van you've got for me?" I jokingly replied. "Best in the garage," he said. Saying our goodbyes, we headed down to the furniture shop to pick up the carpets. Time was of the essence. Loaded up and we left to start our journey down south.

I got as far as Uddingston near Bothwell services, when I noticed the temperature

gauge had started to rise. I kept my eye on it and reluctantly had to pull into the hard shoulder. Checked under the bonnet to see what the water situation was, and it seemed okay. I thought it was not in the red zone, I'll go a bit further and see if it goes. Up. I also noticed the van would not go any faster than fifty mph, and that was with my foot flat to the floor.

A few more miles and the needle was in the danger zone, I had to stop. This time I phoned the hire firm to be answered by the guy that had hired the van to us. "I've had to stop twice the van is overheating. "I think the engine is going to blow and it's going very slow, seems to be losing power and it won't go above fifty," I said. "Oh, that's ok it will be alright, that's normal for that van".

"NORMAL! "I shouted, "I've got to go all the way down to Manchester in a heap of scrap that won't go above fifty, I'm supposed to meet somebody at 2.30 p.m." After a pause he said, "**I'll pray for you**" and hung up before I could reply. The **steam** was coming out of my ears by this time. It was a question of do I take it back, but I had lost so much time I decided to carry on if the fuckin thing blew up it was down to him.

On the way down I had to keep my foot hard to the accelerator sometimes giving my leg a rest from cramping up, by moving over and using my other foot, it was agony, After 4.½ hours we got there and the guy   I was supposed to meet was still there even with us being 1.½ hours late. We decided to go to the 1st house and make a start, we also decided to stay the night in that house, as it gave us more time the next day to work out what area we were going to base our hotel in, as it turned out, all the houses were in different areas.

Anyway after 3 nights in a hotel and successfully completing the other four houses, we made our way back up to Scotland and took it at a slower pace if that was possible to stop my leg from getting cramp. After disposing the rubbish in the back of the van at the local tip.

We returned it back to the garage, where I stormed into the reception room where about four or five people were waiting. The owner was standing there, "nice journey" he said, I fumed "NICE JOURNEY that'll be right 50 mph all the way down to Manchester in that heap of shite" I shouted. "There I told you I'd pray for you, nothing wrong   with

that van, you lie that is a good van" he said. My wife chipped in "don't call my husband a liar" he turned round "you're no lady" he quipped. I threw the van keys on the counter and said to the people sitting there, "if you want to do your flitting today don't take that thing I've just brought back, but if you've any sense you'll get up and walk out." Nobody moved, the lure of a cheap van overrode everything else. We went outside to be met by Sammy the mechanic, "I thought you said that was the best van you had", Sammy replied "**IT IS, IT'S THE ONLY ONE WITH A RADIO**".

ENOUGH SAID I THOUGHT.

I WONDER IF HE'D BE INTERESTED IN THIS LOGO

JUST HIT THEM WITH A HAMMER

A heating job we were doing over in Govan one day early morning 8.00a.m. as usual. We got into the house at the same time as the gas fitters. Now we never look down our noses at anybody. After all I was brought up in a single end in Shettleston the great utopia in the east end of Glasgow, so I have no reason to. Anyway, we started to lift the carpets around the walls that required access for the radiators and piping.

44

The house was not the cleanest we had been in, actually it was a fuckin mess, with old wrappers and empty crisp packets and bits of biscuits all around and under the furniture, of what little they had. I started loosening the living room carpet which didn't have many tacks in it, but over at the fireplace it just pulled back.

I must have given it a sharp tug thinking it was secured because the next minute there was stuff flying all over the place which I thought was dirt or crumbs or something until I realised the crumbs were moving. I shot back trying to rid myself of whatever these things were and making a lot of noise about it. The guy that lived in the house who had been sitting on the couch, got up and grabbed my hammer from me and said,

"I JUST FUCKIN HIT THEM WI A HAMMER", BANG BANG!

45

I didn't need to lift that carpet. It could have walked out the door itself. We were so glad to get out of that house, fortunately we did not have to go back.

IT HAD BEEN FUMIGATED.

CHINESE PUZZLE

Back in the eighties or 1987 to be precise, I started working for myself again and if I remember right. Answer machines had not long appeared. With me being a gadget freak I wanted one. Only this time there was a particularly good reason, I needed it to keep my business ticking over if I was out of the house as my wife was in full time employment, thus no one to answer any calls. Now this answering machine was top of the range at the time, so it was expensive £105.00 to be exact, I always remember because I was not too keen to tell the wife.

47

Anyway, I did, and she was not amused although she didn't say anything, but I could tell as you can if you get that certain kind of look. So, I set it all up as usual not reading the instructions then wondering where is that bit, and what do you do with this bit, I got there in the end. My wife says it is a man thing whatever that means.

Next day I returned to the house wondering if anybody called, and lo and behold the wee red light was flashing. I couldn't wait, I pressed the message button to hear a faint funny sounding kind of voice and just made out the phone number (I had set the machine at a low volume) they had left to return the call regarding fitting a carpet. I immediately phoned the number to be answered by a woman, saying "Is that the carpet fitter I called earlier", "yes" I replied. "I have a big room with some stuff in it that has to be moved, and the carpet might need joining, can you do it". "Yes, I can, depending on how much heat seam tape I will have to use and the size of the room that you said is very large, it will cost £110.00. "OK that's fine you come tomorrow morning". "Yes, I will come about 9.00 a.m. I couldn't wait for my wife to get home to tell her the 1st job I got on the answer machine was going to pay for it.

Arriving at the job the next morning at 9.00 a.m. sharp, I always try to be punctual, it's a trait of mine, a good one I suppose. The address was in Hill St. up near the Art School, a top flat it was. The door was opened by a Chinese man, not the woman I was talking to, I went to walk in, "no downstairs" he said. He opened the door of the lower flat, showed me the room, and left me saying "okay" and went back to the flat upstairs.

I gaped at the scene inside the room, which was large but not as big as what the woman said over the phone. I didn't feel guilty about the price I quoted her, because

49

"SOME STUFF" were the words she used to describe the contents were a joke. The room was half full of cups, saucers, plates, and utensils about fifteen to twenty inches high.

They must have owned a restaurant or a cash and carry and this was their stock. Nothing else but to plod on I thought, it did not need much adaptation, so I didn't use too much seaming tape. I started fitting the carpet about as far as I could before starting the tedious task of shifting all these dishes to the other end of the room on top of the half-fitted carpet. Completing that, I resumed fitting the other half of the carpet.

Now some guys might have finished the job like that, but me being me, I am not like that. So, I started moving all the dishes back to the other end of the room from where they started. Now my wife and I at the time collected antiques and I was very fond of oriental ceramics, but I think it will be a long time before I look at another one. Back to the job, I went upstairs to get paid, and the man said "I come look he opened the door looking at the dishes still in the same place they originally were and exclaimed!

"WOW! HOW YOU DO THAT?!"

and paid me my money.

'I'D LIKE TO THINK I HAD CREATED MY OWN CHINESE PUZZLE"

INSISTENT TILER

Usually approaching Christmas, the demand for fitting carpets tends to get higher, people want to freshen up their decor and furnishings in their homes with the coming new year. I don't know if it's a Scottish thing, but I know the same thing happens at the Glasgow fair holidays, if people were not going away, they would tend to spend money on a new carpet. I told the young guy who had started to work part time with me on weekends, we would probably be working Sundays up until new year.

So, this job was over in the Clarkston area of Glasgow if I remember right. It was one of these old, terraced houses with a long hall and turning stairs as well as a mid-landing, another set of straight stairs before reaching the top landing. There was also a bedroom on the top floor that was being fitted with the same tartan carpet, as well as the dining room on the ground floor. It was a big job and would probably take the best part of the day.

We started doing the preparation tasks, when the man of the house remarked, "I hope it's all going to match", I turned round cutting my finger at the same time, "ow, what do you mean" with the blood starting to drip from my finger. "I want it to match all the way from the dining room up the stairs to the bedroom", he said. I replied, "there is no way that is possible with the dining room and the bedroom carpets already being cut, it would all have to be cut off the one big roll, and even then, it

54

wouldn't have worked". "Why not?" he replied with a raised voice.

By this time, his wife appeared on the scene, to see why he was shouting, "Oh you've cut your finger, come in here and I'll put a dressing on it" she said dragging me into the kitchen away from her man. As she was tending to my finger, her man stormed in shouting **"WHY NOT"**. "Because it's a large pattern repeat, it would have to be replanned and even then, I don't know if it would have been possible with all the turns on the stairs, and if it was, it would take a large amount of carpet," I shouted, "I don't care, I'm a tiler if I can do it so can you "he shouted.

I looked at his wife who appeared to have a sympathetic look and turned round towards him. I replied, "Tell you what if you're so good a tiler, why don't you do it yourself and at the same time, **YOU CAN STICK THE JOB UP YOUR ARSE"**. I packed up my tools and said to the boy that was with me, "c'mon son never mind it's nearly Christmas and we're in high demand, there are plenty more jobs". Leaving the house,

I THOUGHT I HOPE HE DOSEN'T TAKE IT OUT ON HIS WIFE

SHE SAID TAKE IT TO THE DUMP

TINTAWN

We're back to the early days again when I was in partnership with Jimmy, we had been away from Templeton maybe around six months, when a previous work colleague (Wattie) from Templeton asked if he could work for us and learn carpet fitting. We agreed to take him on and give him a chance as we were getting busier. After working with us for a few months we had two jobs booked at the same time, one in Paisley and the other one I think was somewhere in Renfrewshire.

57

The second job was a much bigger job consisting of three carpets, so Jimmy and I were going to do the Renfrewshire one and leave big Wattie, AKA (Walter) to do the Paisley job himself. So the three of us arrived at the Paisley address and carried the carpet up the stairs to the house and into the living room where Wattie was going to fit it.

The carpet in question was a Tintawn Carpet, (HEE HAW), carpeting lasts for donkey's years) used to be the advertising slogan, for those of you who might remember this. It was basket weave type of carpet, and this was the first one that we'd been asked to fit. Anyway we made sure Wattie had everything he needed tools wise as he hadn't acquired his own set of tools yet, and this was the first job he was being left on his own. Satisfied that was the case we left telling him we would probably be back in a couple of hours or so.

Jimmy and I got to our job and proceeded to fit the carpets, a large living room and two bedrooms, which took us a bit longer than we expected as well as the traveling time, it was about three and half hours before we got back to Wattie. He was quite pleased with himself having just fitted his first carpet on his own.

As the house was empty, no furniture, he was just standing there, remarking " what kept you my legs are sore standing about." Jimmy replied *why didn't you sit down on the carpet, Wattie." He replied " It's fuckin sore sitting on that thing, I tried it for a while, but I had to get up. Actually it was fuckin sore fitting it, my knees are all nobbles.

We looked down at the carpet to realise he had fitted it upside down all the knots of the weave were on the surface instead of being on the underside. There was nothing we could do as the room was a funny shape

59

and it wasn't possible to reverse it. We'd just have to leave it and wait for the complaint to come in. You know it never did which we couldn't understand. So all that hype about the carpet lasting for donkey's years must have been true , especially in this case, as it was,

TOO FUCKIN SORE TO WALK ON.

**HEE
HAW**

CHRISTMAS DECORATION

Another private job I remember doing was over in Shawlands. We had just finished completing two homeless flats that I was contracted to do for the furniture shop that I have mentioned before so there were three of us, and the private job in question was just a bedroom carpet to be fitted. We should not all have gone in, but we did. It was a ground floor flat, and the door was opened by a wee woman who invited us into the hall that appeared to have a lot of Chinese lanterns hanging from the ceiling.

I explained that we had just come from a big job and that was why there were three of us. It turned out the bedroom was even smaller than I thought it would be, it really was only a box room about seven feet by twelve feet, so really there was only enough room for myself to fit the carpet. I had only been in there about five minutes when there was a series of knocks at the door. I had to pull the carpet back in order to open it.

It was John my mate and fellow worker, "Tam" he splutters, "you're never going to believe it, I went into the living room to ask the woman for a drink of water" still spluttering, "the place is full of Christmas decorations, ornaments and animals, I could hardly get in the door" still trying to control his hysterical laughter. "Whit "I said it's only the beginning of October, quiet John, she'll hear you."

With John's infectious hysterics it had started aff Wullie the other guy that was with us. "Fucksake will you both shut up? She'll hear you" I shouted whisperingly to them. I got them settled down as I had just finished fitting the carpet, there was a voice at the door, by this time we were all in this wee room trying to keep quiet. "C'mon through into the living room, I've put some tea and biscuits out for you", the woman said.

God, I thought will there be any room for us after what John told me, will I be able to control the two of them. Reluctantly I went through to the living room, with John and Wullie following me. I couldn't believe my eyes, the place full to the brim, lanterns, lights, ornaments, gnomes who must have been brought in for Christmas, or else to avoid the approaching colder weather, Three feet high reindeer, in the bay window, one for each window. And there were more lights, even some stuck up the gnome's arses. I am surprised she managed to find room for us.

"Your decorations are lovely, are you no a wee bit early with them?" I hesitatingly said. "Oh no, they've been up two weeks already, I put them up early because I'm going into hospital next week for a few days. I usually put them up towards the end of October, so I just wanted to be sure", she said.

I could sense the other two with me were struggling to control themselves as I was. "The kids love them every year, coming into the garden and looking at them through the window, but it's when they BASTARDS from the EVENING Paper come round, I don't like. I just tell them to FUCK OFF, but they just keep coming. At that we had to say our goodbyes and make a quick exit before we all burst into laughter

SANTA HAS COME EARLY

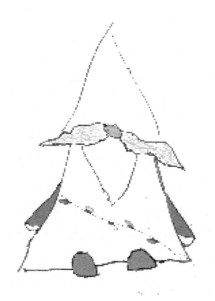

A FAMOUS CASTLE

You'll remember from an earlier story, me telling you about big Wattie, AKA (Walter) from Templeton. Well, this was about ten years later. By this time Wattie was working in his own business which he had started about five years previously. I was going to be emigrating to South Africa in about six weeks' time, and I had finished working in the job I had before a certain date in order to claim my pension contributions back. So, until then Wattie had asked me if I could help him out. He had managed to establish himself with this guy who had contracts

66

with the NHS amongst other places such as Glasgow School of Art and suchlike.

Anyway, this particular job he asked me to help him with was in a famous castle that shall not be named. We arrived to be met by the owner, he knew Wattie's name who he hadn't met before, so he was surprised that he did. Obviously, the company Wattie was working for had told the owner who to expect. He led us inside, it was amazing, suits of armour surrounded us in the entrance hall, with paintings everywhere, and you could feel the sense of history in the building.

"OK men the owner said follow me it's up in the attic, you might be better bringing the carpet in first, save yourselves a double journey, it's quite a trek up the stairs". We nipped out to get the carpet and started following him up the stairs. I can't remember how many floors there were, but I know we were knackered when we got there. "This is it men just move the furniture about as required, I'll leave you to it", he said. The room was a fair size, so there was plenty of room to move stuff about.

There were various things in the room, paintings, a bust, an upright piano and a few small statues, amongst other items. The first thing to get moved was the heavy upright piano, once that had been shifted, it enabled us to start fitting the carpet. As I proceeded with the fitting, various objects were getting moved about, I paused for a second and happened to turn round and look behind me aghast at what I was seeing.

A large canvas oil painting had been placed against a corner of the upright piano, an ominous peak was beginning to form on the canvas, I couldn't imagine the weight and pressure that was being exerted on the canvas, so I shouted to Wattie, "the painting! move it quick, it's going to get damaged" At first Wattie didn't know what I was shouting at him for, then it dawned on him. "Thank god you noticed it", "Noticed it, you couldn't help but notice it"! I shouted.

Disaster averted we carried on, until there was a knock at the door, then slowly, tentatively the door opened. It was the lady of the house, with tea and sandwiches for us, "just a little something to keep you going" she said and left. While we were having our tea and sandwiches   Wattie decided to light up a cigarette, "do you think you should", I said. "Don't see the harm, I'll open the windae and let the smoke out" I thought to leave him to it after all he's in charge of the job, it's his responsibility.

So, we carried on shifting stuff about until we finished the job.   Wattie had one last fag as we were packing our tools up, Wattie said "right that's us", at the same time throwing his cig out the window, which immediately blew straight back in. "Fucksake Wattie, where is it?", I shrieked, with us scrambling to try and sniff out where it was. After what seemed like an eternity, we found it before it burned through anything. I blurted out. "I don't see what all the panic was about", replied Wattie

"YOU DON'T, IT'S A WELL-KNOWN FACT"."THIS PLACE NEARLY BURNT DOON ABOUT SIX YEARS AGO, AND HERE'S YOU TRYING TO DAE IT AGAIN!" I SHOUTED.

ARSEHOLE

It's not the first time I have gone to fit a carpet only to find they had got someone else to do it, probably because they could do it sooner, and not having the decency to phone me to cancel. These occasions usually happened with some people that had responded to my advert in the Evening Times. One such job was in the Cadder area of Glasgow which was about ten miles away and which had taken me roughly twenty-five minutes to get there.

I went up the stairs to the first-floor landing where I found the name I was

72

looking for and pushed the doorbell and waited. I thought they couldn't have heard me, maybe the bell wasn't working so I knocked on the door vigorously. Still no answer, don't tell me I thought, I lowered myself to look through the letterbox, to reveal what looked like a new carpet that had been fitted in the hall. Shit I thought, I've just wasted time and petrol travelling here, reluctantly I walked away back to my car feeling deflated.

Got back to my house with my wife asking, "what's wrong?". "I'm pissed off, a waste of time, nobody there" I replied and proceeded to make myself a coffee. A few days later I got a phone call about fitting a carpet in a caravan in a residential site in Uddingston. I gave the guy a price and agreed a day and time to do it. I took my son Tom with me to give me a hand on the day. It was quite awkward trying to find the caravan on site, but we did. I chapped the door, no answer, chapped again, nothing, by this time I was getting agitated. I looked through the window, "Not again". I had the guy's phone number, tried that to no avail. "Let's go," I said to my son.

I got back to my house and my wife enquired "Well"? ".Don't ask," I said. Later that night I tried to phone this guy again, this time he picked up. "Hi this is the carpet fitter, we were over earlier, and you weren't there, I see you had the carpet fitted" "So what" he replied. "So, what, I've just wasted my time," I said. "Tough" he said, "Oh is that right" I replied at the same time as putting the phone down, saying to my wife **"FUCKIN ARSEHOLE"**. seeing I wasn't getting anywhere when I heard a voice coming from the earpiece, **"I FUCKIN HEARD THAT I KNOW WHERE YOU LIVE"**. Needless to say, we never did hear from him again.

I'VE LEARNED NOW TO MAKE
SURE I'VE PUT THE PHONE DOWN

CARRAZY

This job came to me from a project manager called Jim who I had previously done a couple of jobs for. This is when we were incorporating cleaning carpets and initial cleans in my company. When I say a couple of jobs, the first one was a full four storey building plus caretakers flat on top, in a well-known insurance office that was to be refurbished while occupied from top to bottom. We cleaned the whole building over five nights a floor a night which was no mean task.

Anyway, Jim had got in touch with me, asking if we could come over to the project, he was working on in the grounds of Lennox Castle Hospital, which is Celtic Training Complex now. The work was going on in what I believe used to be the nurse's accommodation. It was being refurbished and turned into a cafeteria downstairs and upstairs there were about ten rooms, which were in a right mess. If I remember right, you could access the upper floor via stairs at either end. The rooms upstairs were in disarray and full of junk.

The previous day my wife was going through them one at a time, and in one of them she found a Strait Jacket that had remnants of blood on it, she called me up to show me it and I can assure you it wasn't a pretty sight, and we told the other ones working with us about it. Anyway Marion was back up there carrying on with what she was doing the day before, meanwhile wee John was working at the bottom of the stairs at the other end of the building with my sister-in-law Margaret using noisy cleaning machines, and belting out Patsy Cline's Crazy, (Pub Singer Style).

Marion felt an uneasiness coming over, her thinking about what she had seen the day before, which was only a couple of doors away from where she was, she decided to get a change of environment by going downstairs, her pace started off slowly but with an urgency beginning to creep in, she started running along the passage and flew through the swing doors with an almighty bang and down the stairs, at which point, the Crazy voices turned to shrieks, with John and Margaret flying out the bottom exit, not knowing what had happened.

A pale faced Marion emerged from the bottom exit apologetically saying, **"SORRY I PANICKED!"** When wee John got his wits back**, "I could have had a heart attack"**, he panted and Margaret chiming in **"And I've wet myself"**.

EVERY TIME I HEAR PATSY CLINE'S CRAZY, THIS STORY COMES TO MIND

CARPET FITTING CLASS

The title of this story refers to the time I went to do this job for an Asian gentleman, who phoned me and asked for a price to fit his large sitting room carpet, I told him how much, and he tried to haggle the price down, "No No No, it doesn't work like that, you tell me size and I tell you a non-negotiable price" I said. Eventually he caved in on the chance that I refused to do it.

Pollokshaws, a well to do area at the time, (I don't know about now) was where the house was located. A Victorian detached mansion, it must have been worth a few

80

bob, no wonder with all that haggling that he must have used in his business dealings. I was shown into the sitting room, which was a large room, I double checked the size to make sure it was the same as I had quoted on, it proved to be right.

Apart from the carpet, which was half a roll of broadloom, forty-four sq. yds in all, the only other item in the room was a large couch, a four-seater, think. I maneuvered the carpet into position and started to partially unroll it as far as where the couch was and proceeded to start fitting the carpet. So, I am working away cutting and banging and at the same time getting the impulse to turn round, you know that strange feeling that someone is watching you.

I gave in and turned round, lo and behold there were six Asian men squeezed onto the four-seater couch, sitting there quietly, I stopped banging, the sound of silence was eerie. "I'm sorry I'll need to be shifting you in a minute so I can fit the carpet at the door" thinking that'll get rid of them, to my annoyance it didn't, they lifted the couch carried up to the other end of the room, turned it round to face me and all squeezed back onto it, all this was done in silence. Good God I thought I'll never get rid of them.

I bit the bullet and carried on till I finished. Went through to the room where the man that had booked me to do the job was and was paid no problem. It was only after I had left the house, I thought if only I had said to my audience:

THAT I WAS GOING TO CHARGE
THEM FOR CARPET FITTING LESSONS,
I MIGHT HAVE GOT RID OF THEM

LARGS

You'll remember my pal Wattie and how I was doing work for him before I went to South Africa, well this was another job I did for him that was linked to that same contract that he did for the guy who had all the NHS work. It was a residential home for children with learning difficulties down in Largs. Wattie had asked me if I could deal with it myself as he was busy with work in Glasgow. He said it was a fair-sized carpet to be fitted in the recreation room, and I would need someone to give me a hand.

The only person that I knew who was available at the time was one of my neighbours whose name was Jim. As he was out of work, he was thankful and agreed to help me, he didn't have any experience fitting carpets and he would only be labouring. Jim was one of these types of guy, that anybody would be hard pushed not to get on with, always a good laugh, he had that kind of personality.

On the day of the fitting, we went to my supplier to get some materials, which included an eight-foot metal bar that I had to flex a little to get it into my car. The journey was a bit uncomfortable for Jim as he had this metal bar coming over his shoulder and jammed underneath the glove compartment. Arriving at the home I walked round the car to Jim's side to remove the metal bar as it was in his way and he had to wait till I took it out, which I started to do and there was a pinging sort of sound followed by OWCH! Jim had been caught with the bar which was under tension and whacked him on the nose. Fortunately, it stopped bleeding, but left him with a cut that ended up being a small scar.

When Jim came to, (I forgot to say he had passed out) we proceeded into the home, what a start and we hadn't even begun. The recreation room was bigger than I was led to believe, this was going to take us a couple of days. Wattie had pulled a fast one on me, the fair-sized carpet he was referring to be a full roll of broadloom. So, nothing else for it but to get stuck in. There was a lot of moving furniture about, desks,chairs,sofas, and cabinets amongst other things. All this plus there some occupants still using room as there was nowhere else for them to go.

There was this wee boy about the age of nine sitting at this angled desk, with what I can only describe as the largest jigsaw I have ever seen. It must have been at least four feet by three feet and maybe about 80% complete. Jim was walking past carrying a large scraping tool which was used to remove the remains of the old carpet from the floor, when it caught the corner of the desk and upended the jigsaw.

There were pieces flying everywhere. Jim was profusely apologetic to the wee boy, he kept repeating himself "Sorry, Sorry," then he must have thought to placate the wee soul, "NEVER MIND SON, AT LEAST YOU'LL BE ABLE TO PUT IT BACK TOGETHER". It was quite innocent the way he said it with no malice intended, with the wee boy looking up at Jim and asking the carer he was sitting with, "How long have I been here?", the wee boy asked. "Two years", She replied, He hesitatingly asked,

"DO YOU THINK I'LL BE HERE IN ANOTHER TWO"

I LOVE YOUR SHOES

Back in the day when we were working with the heating firm that had the council contract, they had houses in a particular area of Darnley that the central heating was being renewed in. The old system was a vented blown air type and was being removed prior to the new one being installed. In these houses we had to lift the carpets the previous day, only to find out they were removing asbestos from the cupboards that had the main heating unit installed in.

The cupboard had been tented off, but to try and lift and remove carpets when the tented area was overlapping on top of the carpet, can't help but leave doubts in our minds did we inhale any of the dust that had supposedly been removed. These houses were pensioner type semi bungalows and this particular one is indelibly stuck in my memory.

We rang the doorbell and waited for a man to appear at the door. "We're here to lift your carpets" I said, the man just turned away and started to mozy along the hall when my wife pointed at his feet. I thought he was wearing brown slippers, but he was leaving footprints on the carpet, only then did I realise his feet were covered in shite. "Right, I said, we'll have to phone the office mister, just shut your door".

Getting to the van, I was on the phone to them right away, "The carpet is covered in shite, I think it's all over the house, we're not going in" I said. After about three or four days, we returned to finish the job. The place had been thoroughly cleaned. What you have to do to make a living.

IT HAD LEFT AN INDELIBLE
IMPRINT IN MY BRAIN

HELLO LOVE

We have travelled all over Scotland on some of these contracts and this job was down in Sanquhar in the Dumfries and Galloway region. As usual we were down there in plenty of time ahead of the scheduled start time of 8.00 am. These jobs were being done the same day as the heating installation. As we drove into the village trying to find the street we were looking for, while looking at the map, we saw that it was a maze of streets we had to negotiate through to reach our given address.

93

As we started to make our way along the road, a man signalled us to stop. "Where are you going?" he enquired. We told him, "you've got a problem, there's a big bull running about up there", he enthused. "Thanks, we'll look out for it," I said. Cautiously we turned a few corners and there it was, a big brute of a thing, staring at us.

This was the street that our job was in, and according to the house numbers I could see the one we wanted was beyond where the bull was. Christ, I thought, what are we going to do. It must have been an answer to my prayers, a wee wummin came out of her house and started shouting at the bull,

"C'mon Angus whit are you daeing oot", grabbed him by his nose ring and led him towards a gate at the top of the street. I couldn't believe it; she was the height of nothing. As she disappeared into the distance, we approached the door of the house. It was one of those half-glazed doors with frosted glass and gave it a good chap.

A blonde appeared behind the glass with long straight hair from what I could see, as she opened the door, I quipped, "Good morning love carpet fitters", to be confronted by this blonde who had the most beautiful straight hair and a beard. "Aye whit is it"? with a gruff voice as I slowly started to sink into myself, whimpering "Sorry I thought you were a woman", shut up I thought you're making it worse.

It seemed to take forever to finish and get out of there. When we went back to relay the carpets, the blonde image appeared behind the door again, I thought oh god here we go again, only to be opened by a woman with long straight blonde hair, his wife

I thought that's how they must have got together as they had a lot in common.

CLASSIC CAR

The job on this particular day over in Govan did not seem to be any different or out of the ordinary than any other heating job except for the odd exception. You might think as you're halfway through the book, this guy has had a helluva lot of exceptions. Anyway, we went into the house ahead of the heating engineers, we started in the hall and progressed through to the bedrooms leaving the living room to the end.

When we did eventually go into the living room, the man who was sitting on a chair at the fire said, "Watch you don't damage my car!". "What do you mean?" I replied. He was getting a bit frustrated with me, "My motor!" he shouted, Now I don't know how we missed it but on the wall past the window was the front half of a full-sized Ford Anglia as if it had crashed through the wall. God, is that real?" I asked. "Of course, it is, It's mine, I used to drive it back in the late sixties,

I've had it fae new, until the engine packed up, the logbook and everything else is in the glove compartment," he said. "Oh right, so it's the shell then" I said. "Naw Naw son, the engine is still in it; everything still works apart fae the engine" he enthused. "Wow what do you mean everything still works" I said. " Och wait and I'll show you" he replied. He lifted a remote control, pressed a button and the lights came on. "That's great," I said. He pressed another button and the indicators started flashing, and before I could say anything else.

98

He quipped, getting a bit cocky, "wait and see this'', pressing another button and music (Hi Ho Silver Lining), started emanating from the front grill of the Anglia, "that's the original radio, it's still in the dash". "How did you manage to do all that?" I asked." Och that's nothing" he replied, I fitted a graphic equalizer to it and the wipers go to the beat" demonstrating it by pressing another button. Sure, enough the old wipers started enthusiastically dancing to the beat and a graphic equalizer appeared behind the grill. "That's brilliant, thanks for showing us," I said, and we finished off lifting the carpet. When we got outside the heating engineers asked

"What kept you" looking at us bewilderingly, I quipped,

"DON'T ASK HIM TO ABOUT HIS ANGLIA YOU'LL BE THERE AW DAY."

TV SHY

I had a contract with a furniture/bedding manufacturer, doing various jobs that they had managed to procure. One such job was in Rosyth Naval Base where we were stripping out the old carpets and refitting new ones on a RFA (Royal Fleet Auxiliary Ship) where a lot of refitting was going on, so it was a very busy ship. Because of the size of the work involved I had recruited four extra workers on a self-employed basis.

So, it was all hands-on deck, excuse the pun. We were fitting out all the cabins approximately about twenty, plus the officers' mess. This included cleaning some furniture, so water had to be carried up the gangway to the various decks, which could only be accessed by climbing up ladders as the stairs had been removed, time consuming it was.

One of the days we were in the cabins laying underlay, one of the guys (Stuart) who was partially lying under a bunk bed fitting the felt when one of the dock workers walked past him and remarked "hello darling". Stuart who had long straight black hair, emerged from under the bed shouting "I'm naebody's' fuckin darling specially no yours, do you think your being fuckin funny?".

The dock worker scurried off shouting a muffled "SORRY" and disappeared down the ladders to safety. Stuart who by this time, whose face was pure red, quipped "I'll need to get this fuckin haircut, I'm fed up, this happens aw the time, I'm pissed aff". A voice came from one of the other cabins "never mind you can still pull them". Stuart erupted "who fuckin said that?" A cabin door slammed shut never to be opened again until the safety of the tea break. Stuart never did find out who owned the voice.

For our tea breaks and lunch break we would head to the canteen, on the quayside. This particular day, we were on our lunch break and this TV camera crew came into the canteen and I have never seen so many people ducking under tables or disappearing behind newspapers, obviously a lot of these self-employed and part time workers did not want to be TV stars.

Sure enough, that night on STV 6.00 pm news it was on, there for all to see **if you**

knew what you were looking for, people picking up supposedly dropped coins, tipped bunnets, plenty of Daily Express readers, which was the biggest daily newspaper you could get. It was even good for two people reading it at the same time.

AS I SAID IF YOU KNEW WHAT LOOKING FOR

THE SALAD BOX

A heating job we had when we worked in the Dumbarton area, was situated in a two up two down semi. A man opened the door to us and beckoned us in after explaining what we were there for. After finishing the lower floor, we started in the hall, and I remarked to my wife about the grey coloured carpet on the stairs.

On closer inspection, there wasn't a carpet there, it was covered in a thick dust, layers of it. It was that thick you could mistake it for grey felt, it appeared to be woven, a crafter could probably have used it for felting. So, after tiptoeing up the stairs to the bedrooms which had no carpets but large rugs and linoleum surrounds and masses of vegetables and fruit everywhere. In the wardrobes and in the chest of drawers which were in the open position probably to aerate them.

The floor was covered in plastic supermarket baskets, stacked on top of one another, that was just one room. The second room could not be any worse, but it was, you couldn't even see the window, maybe he did not want any light in order to preserve veg and fruit while longer. The place was covered in dust. So really there was nothing for us to do in this house as the downstairs had rugs and floorboards as well.

We said to the man about the amount of produce he had and did he have an allotment. "Och aye, I sell it doon the market every week and round the doors, here 's one of my cards, if you ever need any, I deliver anywhere" we thanked him and said our goodbyes.

I COULDN'T HELP THINKING TRADING FROM HERE WAS A BIT OF A GREY AREA

THE SALAD BOX

GOING UP

This is another story about my pal Wattie. You may remember he was the guy that used to work in Templeton carpet factory, he was telling me about what happened to him on this job that he was doing in an office in Glasgow city centre. I think it was his accountant who had referred him to one of his clients and it was quite a big job. Wattie had a fair amount of equipment and could handle fair sized jobs.

I had hired some machines from him the time I landed my first big cleaning job. He

109

had one of his usual would-be apprentices with him. I kept telling him all he was doing was breeding cowboy carpet fitters and more competition for himself. What I did not like was in later years it would develop into competition for me as well. Anyway, he would never listen and just carried on regardless. I also told him it would come back to bite him in the bum someday.

So Wattie and his companion got to their job and started offloading his equipment. I don't know if this happened at the beginning of the job or whether he was into it a couple of days, but as they moved machines upstairs, to save time, the guy that was with him was sending stuff up in the lift to Wattie who was on the second floor. His first load went up successfully, no problems. It was the second consignment that this occurred.

He had loaded the lift with buckets, water carriers and the biggest cleaning machine that Wattie owned. Shouting up the lift shaft to Wattie "that's them, I'm sending them up" as he closed the door and pressed the lift button, only to see a cable with plug sticking through the door slowly rising above him and see it start to strain against the door and grind to a halt. Wattie heard the noise, shouting down, "what's happened it's stopped", "I'm not sure," shouted his workmate.

Wattie bolted down the stairs to find him standing staring at a plug at the lift door which was about level with the ceiling. "Fucksake, what am I going to do" screams Wattie, "see if there is a phone number for a lift engineer anywhere". "Usually there is one inside the lift," said the workmate. "Well, that's nae fuckin use" shouts Wattie.

There were no clues who to phone and this was a night shift they were doing; he would have to wait till morning before he could contact anybody. Next morning, he phoned the person in charge who by this time had found out it wasn't working. They had to get a specialist lift engineer up from England to fix it. I think it cost Wattie about £1800 through his insurance.

SO IT CAME BACK TO BITE HIM IN THE BUM

KNIGHTSWOOD BRANCH

Nowadays the trend seems to be if it is not paying, then shut it down, such as is the case with banks especially in small towns and villages such as the one I live in. You could be subsidising these banks with your hard-earned money that you may have struggled to save and receiving very little or no interest to speak of, yet you may still have to travel ten miles or so to use their services if you're not internet savvy.

Back in the nineties this was not the case in one specific area a new branch was opened in Knightswood, only this one was under a woman's carpet, she didn't even

114

know one had been opened there. This is how the story goes, it was another heating job we were doing, as usual we went in first at 8.00 am with gasfitters sitting outside in their vans. I started to lift the carpet in the living room while my wife proceeded to loosen the hall carpet.

After about four or five minutes my wife called me to come and see something, I thought she had come across a phone cable or an electrical wire, which used to happen quite often. It's amazing what some people put under their carpets, only this time it wasn't either. it was an open envelope containing money, £600.00 to be exact, you may think nosy bastards, which was not the case, it was marked on the outside, and also to safeguard ourselves, I made it a policy of anything like that, to count it and someone to witness it, so we can't be accused of taking anything, if the persons says it was more.

115

So, we shouted to the woman who was upstairs to come down and see what we had found. When she saw it, and we told how her much it was, her cheeky response was "Where did you get that?" in a raised voice. My wife replied "I found it under the hall carpet" "That old bastard (meaning her dead husband) must have put it there, he was forever fixing that carpet, it kept coming away at the door" she retorted. We finished up, not a word of thanks not nothing. We went outside and told the gasfitters what we had found to keep ourselves right.

Next day when we went back, still no thanks to my wife, all she did was moan about the mess and the dust, as if new central heating can be installed and not leave a trace. When we saw the gasfitters later that day, they asked if she had given my wife anything, "Nothing, not even a box of chocolates, old bastard" they said.

UNGRATEFUL OLD BUGGER I THOUGHT, SHE DIDNAE EVEN HAVE TO TRAVEL TEN MILES TO GET IT.

CELEBRITIES

I have done a few jobs over the years for celebrities, but this job out in Falkirk beats the lot. It was the CSA building (Child Support Agency) in the Callendar Park area of Falkirk. It was a brand-new build, and when we arrived there the gable end was being rebuilt, as it had suffered storm damage. Jim the clerk of works I knew phoned us to ask if we could come out and do some initial cleaning and as it turned out various other things. Basically, it was to clean up behind any kind of mess left by the builders.

118

We had brought everything I thought we would need to tackle the tasks in hand, etc. cleaning machines, floor scrubbers, chemicals, various brushes, and two sets of step ladders. Arriving on site I searched out Jim, who then took me on a tour of the building, showing me what he wanted done. It was a much bigger job than I was led to believe, fortunately I was able to jiggle other jobs on our books about a bit. I could see us being here at least a week.

One of the things I remember happening was an electrical company that was working there as well as us. I think there must have been about three or four electricians, and they were working throughout the building.

One of them kept taking our step ladders to work inside the ceiling without asking and I was getting pissed off, and the last time he did it I thought enough is enough, I went to where he was working and removed the ladders. I had no regrets in doing it but

119

when I found out he was stuck up there for over an hour, until one of his workmates had heard his cries for help, I did feel a wee bit of remorse, but not much.

On the third day we were there, they had introduced a book in the reception area which you had to sign in and out. One of the jobs Jim had asked us to do was operate a cherry picker, which I had to renege on as I'm not too good with heights. It was when I signed in the next morning, I noticed Marilyn Monroe had signed in before me, and in front of her was JFK. "What the fuck I thought, I'm working with famous people. As the week went on, I think the whole of the Equity Union was working here. But the one that topped the lot was one night we were working late, and we were the only ones left on the job and as we were signing out, the last signature before us was

ELVIS HAS LEFT THE BUILDING.

THEY'LL NO BE LONG

Another time when we were down working in Manchester again comes to mind. We had just finished fitting out three houses over the last three days. We were just leaving that morning and with a long journey ahead of us I said to the wife "I better fill up with fuel as we're half full and not enough to get us up the road." "Aye" was her reply. So, I pulled into the first garage I came to, thinking I better remember and put diesel in this, as it was a hired van we had again, and my own van used petrol.

I filled the tank up with enough diesel in order to return the van with approximately what had already been in it. I went over to the shop to pay for it and asked one of the two women behind the counter if I could use their toilet. "No problem, but you'll have to wait, someone's already using it," she said. I stood and waited for what must have been about getting near ten minutes, at least that's what it felt like.

"Are you sure somebody is using it?" I asked. "Oh yes it's a family that is using it, just go round, they must be nearly finished" she replied. I looked over to the van and signalled to my wife that I was going round the back of the building. I made my way round the back and sure enough, a car was parked there with two or three people in it and one sitting on the bonnet. "Where's the toilet?" I asked. "Oh, there's somebody in it, oh wait there they are coming out" they replied.

I headed over to the toilet and the woman was good enough to hold the door open for me, "Thanks" I said and went in closing the door behind me. When I finished, I flushed the cistern and went over to the sink to wash my hands. It was only when I went to exit, that I saw it, there was no handle on the door, it was missing. "Fer Fucksake" I shouted, "what am a gonnae dae, fer fucksake" as my blood pressure was beginning to rise. I worked out my bearings and I guessed the main wall in the toilet was the adjoining wall to the shop where the counter was. I started battering the wall as hard as my fists would let me, repeatedly I hit that wall to no avail.

Whit noo I thought and I'm looking at the door to where the handle should have been if I could get something to fit in there to turn it. Looking around scouring every nook and cranny in that toilet, I couldn't see anything, and then **EUREKA!** I spotted it, if I can break a bit safely aff that bracket that's holding up the cistern that might work. I carefully used all the force that I could use without damaging It, got it, the cistern wobbled a wee bit, but it still was hanging on.

I turned towards the door handle with determination that this was going to work.

Did it fuck, it broke, "fucksake" I screamed. There was only one thing left I could do, above the sink was a small window, it was one these wee metal framed ones that open outwards about four or five inches. If I can get up, I'll be able to shout out. Will the sink take my weight, looking at the rusty bit I broke off the cistern, nothing else fur it, I'll need to try? I managed to climb on top of the sink warily to reach the window, thank Christ I thought.

Now the window was just below the ceiling, so I had to creak my neck to line my mouth up with the window. **"HELP, HELP,**

HELP," I was shouting to no avail, my neck was getting sore, I'll have to gie myself a break. I looked at my watch. I've been here twenty minutes, "fucksake" the sink started to creak, please don't, I thought. Has my wife fell asleep in the van, I thought I heard someone walking on gravel, quick back up to the window, another creak,creak from the sink, "fuckit I don't care," looks out and I see my wife turning away to go back around the corner, trying to push my face out the window as far as I could, **"HELP! HELP! MARION HELP!** she kept walking, **"FUR FUCKSAKE MARION"** , it must have been extra volume in my voice through desperation, she stopped and turned round. "Is that you Tom?", "fuck who else wid it be I shouted" She came to the door and turned the handle that was on the outside. "Good God did you no wonder where I was? I was at the end of my tether" I blurted out. "I thought you were constipated," she pleaded.

126

I stormed round to the shop at the front, the two women were there, "hi" one of them said. **"HI?"** I said in a raised voice, "did you not wonder where I was?", my van has been sitting there for about half an hour. I have been locked in the toilet, there's no handle in the inside of the door". "Oh I forgot about that, somebody is coming to fix it" she said and at the same time the other woman

started to slowly disappear under the counter. She looked down and said to the hiding woman "you phoned the locksmith? didn't you". There was no reply, I chipped in,

"YOU BETTER TELL YOUR PAL TO PHONE A PLUMBER AT THE SAME TIME, THE CISTERN AND THE SINK ARE FUCKED" AND STORMED OUT

SANTA

I used to do a lot of work for two brothers who owned a well-known bathroom supplier and installation company that had three different branches, two in Glasgow and later opened one in Ayr. At first it was just local to Glasgow until the Ayr branch opened, which meant I had to do a bit more travelling. I used to do this on a part time basis so with the extra travel I decided to stop doing it. Before I finished working for them,

I fitted a carpet in one of the brothers houses and while I was there, I met his wife who owned a ballet school business in Glasgow, Sheila, we'll call her because I can't remember what her name was. After I completed the carpet installation, she offered me a cup of tea. This was when she told me she ran a ballet school and where it was.

At the time I think I was about fifty-seven, so when she asked me if I would be prepared to step in and be Santa for her ballet school Christmas parties. Christ I must be looking older than I feel I thought. "You're joking" I said, "No, would you? please," she asked. So, if at the time I had said let me think about it, I would have said no, but I didn't, I think I felt a bit pressured into doing it. "Yes" I said reluctantly. "When is the party" I said, "The Saturday before Christmas, oh and it's two parties the same afternoon, one for the tots and one for the older ones" she replied.

God what have I let myself in for I thought. "OK alright, what time have I got to be there for?" I asked, "1.30 pm the first one then the second is 3.00 pm, so you can go for a cup of tea in between" she replied. The day of the party arrived. I was dreading it. I'm sorry I agreed, but too late I thought. When my wife and I arrived there, we were met by Sheila, "Great, come in here and I'll give you your Santa suit". I put it on, I was the skinniest Santa I had ever seen. It was party time and the first of the kids was shown in, I was terrified, felt intimidated by these wee tots, what do I say to them apart from the usual stuff, making a lot of promises not knowing if they'd be kept.

After seeing six or seven of them, it was over. Going outside for a cup of tea minus the Santa suit, my wife enquired "How was it?" "Terrifying and that's only the first part" I replied. We went back to the ballet school for the second party, and the kids were shown in, only this time they were all together. I started off with the younger ones going through the routine I had established, and hearing whispers coming from the older ones who must have been about eleven or twelve, he's not a real Santa, look at him he's dead skinny

When it's your turn ask him where Rudolph is. Did he leave him in the zoo because there's nae snow fer his sledge? I'll ask him wis he on a diet and could the elves no come because they don't work on a Saturday. Oh, aye and ask him for a White Christmas then he'll be able to use his sledge and tell him he'll not be able tae wear his trainers. That is the last thing I remember as I buzzed through them and got to hell out of there... I WASN'T CUT OUT TO BE A SANTA,

INSTEAD OF HO HO HO

IT WOULD BE NO NO N

133

SHOCKER

I used to do a lot of work for a company that had a chain of babywear shops, who I choose to remain nameless. Actually, I think they no longer exist. I used to supply and fit the carpets throughout their chain of shops. Quite often I had to chase them up for my money, which was getting more common with the bigger companies I did work for. On one occasion I was working in their branch that used to be in Wishaw.

I cannot remember if it was a new acquisition or if it was an old one that was getting refurbished, or a complete

134

makeover. When we arrived with the carpet there were painters just finishing off the final touches. Also, an electrician was working away, installing a new fuse box and various fittings as well as new floor sockets. As it was late morning when we arrived, It was obvious we wouldn't be able to finish the job till the next day.

So, I asked the electrician, if he would be finished with the floor sockets for us coming back the next morning. "Aye nae problem, I'm going out just now so if you're going away, just shut the door behind you, I've got the keys. Somebody will open up for you tomorrow" he said. I kept thinking I could smell alcohol from him, as I was in close proximity to him. Anyway, we left. It was later after I arrived home, I went over to the local chip shop to get something to eat, and who staggered out, but the electrician that was working in the shop earlier on.

I was surprised as I didn't know he came from around where I lived, I said "Hi", but he didn't recognise me. We went back the next day, sure enough someone had opened the door for us and must have gone away as the shop was empty, so we started where we left off. As we progressed towards where the checkouts were going to be, it was clear he had not finished the floor sockets; it was just the cable sticking through the floor. I had to cut a hole in the carpet in order to pull the cable through, **BANG!** I was thrown back about four or five feet.

When I got myself together, I exclaimed the "wee bastard never isolated the power to these floor sockets". Another hour and we had the job finished. After I dropped the guys off, I phoned the office of the baby shop company to speak to the main man. "That wee electrician never switched the power off to where these floor socket cables are coming through the floor. I was

136

thrown back, I could have been killed, I told him last night that I would be working there next morning, I think I could smell alcohol off his breath at the time, I saw him again later that night coming out of a chip shop, and he looked drunk", I said in a raised voice.

The shop owner asked, "Is that you finished there?". "Aye" I replied. "Well come over and I'll pay you right now" he said. I went to the HQ, and he came down right away to reception, cash in hand. I was usually paid by cheque, that is quickest I have ever been paid. That was the last job I ever did for them.

I TAKE IT, IT WAS TO INFLUENCE ME NOT TO SUE THEM.
AS I HAD NO PROOF

SELL THE VAN

When work quietened off a bit, with one of the companies losing a big contract, I felt that I did not require my long wheelbase Transit, as well as it is having done a fair bit of mileage on the clock and things needing done to it. It was either another van which I didn't really need, or a new car. I decided to opt for the latter. So, I put the van up for sale knowing it needed money to be spent on it.

One of the things was the steering was stiff as hell, and a fair bit of muscle was required to turn it. I advertised it at a fair price taking this into account. After a while I got a response. The guy that came to see it wanted a test drive, I told him about the steering and what was needed to fix it.

He drove it out of the driveway and turned the steering wheel, remarking how stiff it was, I told him it was the stub joints that were causing it. Back to the house we went after about five minutes, that was enough to put him off. After about a month with no other enquires I dropped the price £50.00. I said to one of my friends at the time I had put it up for sale and was having trouble selling it.

"I know a guy who would probably take it off your hands" he said. "Who is that?" I asked. "Oh he's got a garage up near the Will's factory, and has got a lot of vans,

I'm sure he'd be interested in yours", he replied. "You don't mean that big bastard that hires the vans out" I said. "Aye that's right, he hires them out, do you not like him?", he asked. "No, I don't", I said, then proceeded to tell him the story about my long trip to Manchester, "So you can forget it, he can stick his vans up his arse, I wouldn't sell to him if he was the last man standing" I replied.

I sat with the van for about another month or so and out of the blue, the phone rang, it was somebody enquiring about the van. "Aye it's about your Transit, have you still got it?" the caller asked enthusiastically. "Aye I have, would you like to come and see it", I asked. "No, I stay in Springboig, just bring it over, I don't think your far from me, going by your phone number," he said. Now I wasn't wanting to drive over there to be turned down after he tried to drive it. I started telling him all the things that were wrong with it, stiff steering, stub pins needing renewed and wee bit of rust.

"Are you sure you don't want to come over and test drive it?" I said, thinking please come and see it. "No" he repeated giving me his address at the same time. "Where are you coming from? "he continued. "Not far, I'll see you in about half an hour," putting the phone down. I said to my wife that I thought I was wasting my time, but I dug out all the documents and headed over there.

Arriving at the house I walked up the pathway and rang the doorbell. This bloke opened the door, the first thing that struck me was the size of the scar that ran down his face, from just below his eye to his lower jaw. Trying not to look at the scar, "It's about the transit you phoned about" I warily said. "Aye c'mon in, long MOT?" he queried. "Aye, seven months left on it, do you want a wee drive in it?" I asked. "No that's alright, £600.00 you said" he quipped, and he started counting £20.00 notes from a wad that he took from his pocket.

142

I showed him all the documents and repeated myself about the stiff steering and all the other things that were wrong with it, handing him the keys at the same time. "Do you want to come out and look at it and I'll show you how to open the back door as it's a wee bit stiff. "No bother mate, thanks for bringing it over" and ushered me out the door, "Cheer's mate" he said as he closed the door. I went down the road looking for a taxi. On my return to the house in disbelief at what just happened.

WAS HE GOING TO USE IT FOR A ROBBERY, OR DID THAT FRIEND OF MINE TELL THAT BASTARD IN THE GARAGE ABOUT IT AND HE PUT THE GUY UP TO IT.

I'LL NEVER KNOW, I NEVER HEARD FROM THAT GUY AGAIN

CASTLEMILK VIADUCT

This was another one of those fitting jobs that we did for Coulter's shop in Castlemilk. It was a living room and a hall carpet. We fitted the living room carpet first and then proceeded into the hall. We had a look at the clearance of the front door and told the man that we could fit the carpet up to where the door could open freely and trim the carpet so that when he got the door cut, he could tack it down himself or he would have to pay us for coming back.

The other option was to take the door off and get someone to cut it while we were fitting the carpet. "I'll need to get it aff and cut it, before the wife gets back" he said. Seemingly she was at the bingo. He got a hold of a screwdriver and removed the door taking it into the living room. He then disappeared out the front door and down the stairs, next we could hear him chapping one of his neighbours' doors. He came back up the stairs brushing past us carrying tools.

We carried on fitting the carpet to the sound of whining, sawing, the odd crashing noise, and him cursing in that sort of order coming from the living room. We had started fitting at the front door end of the hall to stay out of his road, so when he brought the door out, he could fit it. He was trying to get it back on before his wife got back from the bingo. We were almost finished when he hurried past us with the door and started to hang it back on.

146

He had just got it back on and we heard him saying "I think that's her coming up the stairs, grabbing his tools and disappearing back down to his neighbours passing his wife on the stairs, "I'm just taking these back" he said to her. She came into the house saying "Hi" to us as she passed on her way into the living room. "Fer fucksake what's happened in here" she shouted.

We looked inside, there was sawdust, and wood splinters everywhere and bits of broken wally dug, "That was my favourite, whit the fuck was he daeing" she shouted. "Cutting the front door" we replied. She came out into the hall and looked at the front door, **"Whit the fuck is that The Glenfinnan Viaduct"** she shouted again "You could fuckin limbo under it, that man is fuckin hopeless".

We went into the hall and sure enough, you could feel the draught blowing under the door, which had about an inch gap under it. He cut it short and must have started by drilling holes and then sawing along to join them together and by all accounts it did resemble a viaduct. We left the woman ranting and raving, we didn't see her man.

HE MUST HAVE BEEN HIDING
IN HIS NEIGHBOURS

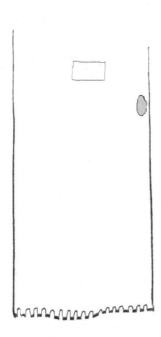

LET ME OUT OF HERE

Remember my pal Wattie, well this is a wee story he conveyed to me when he was alive, sadly he passed away before his time. He was thinking of new ways to expand his cleaning business when he came up with the idea of branching into pest control which was very lucrative, to try and generate extra income. I remember him telling me it was one of the first jobs if not the first he had done.

He got a phone call from a woman in Newton Mearns to come and get rid of a wasp nest in her garage, Wattie responded

"No problem missus, I'll be there within the hour. When I think of it now, it must have been his first job because he didn't have any equipment.

So, he turned up at the woman's house, she eagerly opened the door, "Oh thanks for coming so quick, wait and I'll show you where it is," she said Opening the garage door slightly she pointed in the direction of the nest. "Right leave it with me, I'll just get my equipment out of the van, just you go and make yourself a cup of tea", said Wattie, he didn't want her to see that he didn't have anything special with him.

"I'll just wait for you to go in," the woman said. Wattie gets a big bag and a technical looking box out of the van and goes into the garage with the woman closing the door behind him. He opens his technical looking box and removes a can of Fly spray. Now I don't know if it is the same kind of stuff that you can get now that can destroy the

151

nest from a distance, but Wattie told me that all he had was fly spray as things were tight and that was all he could afford.

The plan was spraying all the nest and run like fuck outside, but unfortunately, when he tried to escape, he could not, the woman had locked the door. Believe it or not, after shouting and battering the door for longer than he wanted to, he managed to escape without getting stung, turns out the only one that got stung was the woman.

"That's it done missus, just leave it a couple of days before you go back in. The woman paid him; I think the going rate then was about £40.00 that's what the council used to charge.

NOW YOU CAN QUITE SAFELY REMOVE ONE OF THESE NESTS FOR ABOUT £5 or £6

CAREFUL

The heating company we were working for was very busy and some days they had three heating installations going on daily. As they all started at the same time, that being 8.00 am, it was impossible to be there on time without holding them back. It was usually two jobs a day which we could cope with. So, on the odd occasion when we had to loosen or lift the carpets the day before and this was one such occasion.

The job in question was over in Rutherglen, a typical ground floor four in a block house. We arrived there in the

154

afternoon and after ringing the doorbell, it was answered by a man with a white stick who was obviously blind. "Good afternoon sir, we're from the heating firm to loosen your carpets, for the gasfitters who are coming tomorrow" I said. Turning round, "Okay in you come" he said, and Started sort of feeling his way along the hall.

It was only after I started loosening the threshold bars at the doors, thinking how stupid I am, doing this he'll end up tripping over something. I said to my wife, "This is crazy it's an accident waiting to happen" and she agreed. We secured everything we had touched and told the man we would be back the next morning early. The gasfitters on the other job's tomorrow will just have to wait, I thought.

Next morning, we got there, and the gasfitters were waiting outside, Archie and his brother George. Archie asked if we were not supposed to have gone there the day before. "The man's blind I said we couldn't lift the carpets, he would have tripped up or something," I said. So being stuck for time I went to the man's door ten minutes earlier than I should have, he answered and let us in.

We made a start in the hall and got all the door bars up. By this time, the gasfitters came in and started to do what they normally do. It so happened this job was a bit different for them also, as the kitchen wall cupboards had to be shifted for the combi boiler, they usually don't have to do this. Anyway, I'm working in the living room, Archie is making a lot of noise in the kitchen, removing the cupboards, then silence, then Archie erupts, "Tom come through here quick!", he shouts. I went through and he is holding up a pile of Penthouse magazines, shouting,

WHEN DID THEY START FUCKIN DAEING THESE IN BRAILLE?!

GLOSSARY

GLASWEGIAN SLANG

AFF :::::::OFF

AW :::::::::ALL

AWA::::: AWAY

AYE:::::::::YES

CANNAE::::CAREFUL or CAN'T

COMIN::::::: COMING

DAE or DAEING:::::: DO or DOING

DINNAE: DON'T

FAE::::::::::: FROM

FUR:::::::::: FOR

GIE or GIESIT::::::::: GIVE or GIVE ME IT

ISIT::::::::::: IS THAT RIGHT or CORRECT

IT'S NO MINE::::::: IT DOESN'T BELONG TO ME

MITHER::::: MOTHER

NAE or NAW: NO

OOT::::::OUT

WHIT::::: WHAT

WID::::::: WOULD

WIDNAE::::::: WOULDN'T

WINDAES::::::: WINDOWS

WI or WIE::::::: WITH

WEANS::::::::: CHILDREN

WRANG:::::::: WRONG

WUMMIN::::::: WOMAN

Printed in Great Britain
by Amazon

11064306R00098